What Are They Saying about Jesus?

by
Gerald O'Collins, S.J.

PAULIST PRESS
New York/Ramsey/Toronto

ACKNOWLEDGMENTS

The first four chapters of this book were published in *The Way*, a quarterly review of contemporary Christian spirituality, published by the English Jesuits, under the titles: *Jesus in Current Theology I* and *II* appearing in the issues of October 1976 (Vol. 16, No. 4) and January 1977 (Vol. 17, No. 1). They are reprinted by permission. In somewhat different form the Appendix appeared in *New Blackfriars* (April 1976), *America* (December 20, 1975), and *The Tablet* (December 20, 1975).

Library of Congress
Catalog Card Number: 77-70640

ISBN: 0-8091-2017-8

Published by Paulist Press
Editorial Office: 1865 Broadway, New York, N.Y. 10023
Business Office: 545 Island Road, Ramsey, N.J. 07446

Printed and bound in the
United States of America

Contents

Preface

The Second Vatican Council (1962-65) gave its attention to ecclesiastical issues. It produced a range of documents on the Church, ecumenism, the liturgy, relations with other religions, the roles of bishops, priests, religious and laity, missionary activity and the rest. But only secondarily did it consider Christology or doctrines about Jesus Christ.

The twelve years since the closing of the Council have shown that any efforts to renew the Church will remain spiritually empty, emotionally hollow and doctrinally unsound unless they draw inspiration and strength from the founder of Christianity himself. If Vatican III were to meet in late 1977, its major document would not be 'The Church in the Modern World', but some response to the question: Who is Jesus Christ for us today?

Theologians and exegetes would have prepared the way for such a document from Vatican III. During the last decade both academic and popular studies have moved beyond the classic Christology which the creeds and councils of early Christianity shaped for well over a thousand years. One thinks of works by Leonardo Boff, Raymond Brown, Christian Duquoc, Hans Frei, Walter Kasper, Hans Küng, Jürgen Moltmann, Wolfhart Pannenberg,

Karl Rahner, John Robinson, Edward Schillebeeckx, Piet Schoonenberg, and the whole group
who have continued to contribute to the 'new quest'
for the historical Jesus. I am putting aside scruples
here and pulling in names almost at random. But
these and other authors serve to illustrate the shift
since 1965. They all seek to provide fresh insights in
answering the question: 'Where and how do we encounter Jesus Christ today?'[1]

At every level, more and more Church leaders,
theologians and other Christians have to come to
recognize a basic truth. Ecclesiastical questions will
never be resolved unless we push further back to our
understanding of Jesus himself. What we *do* with the
Church will rest ultimately on what we *think* about
Jesus.

This book covers several areas. First of all, I
plan to indicate six themes in classical Christology
that no longer satisfy and have prompted the search
for new approaches. This classical Christology was
essentially based on the Council of Chalcedon (A.D.
451), which provided the Church with its traditional
account of Jesus Christ as one person in two natures.
Then two chapters will discuss some key characteristics of recent views. The final chapter argues that
popular writers may express more vividly something
obscured at times by the scholars—the religious appeal of Jesus. Finally, an Appendix contains an ex-
ploratory study on the imagination of Jesus.

In the course of the book I pay particular attention to the 'big three' Jesus-books from 1974:

Kasper's *Jesus der Christus*, Küng's *Christ sein* and Schillebeeckx's *Jezus*. Admittedly Küng takes Christian theory and practice for his topic. But the book spends well over three hundred pages on Jesus Christ —the one who ultimately makes Christianity different from the theory and practice of all other religions and ideologies. In late 1976 Collins (London) and Doubleday (New York) published a translation under the title *On Being a Christian*. Shortly before that, Paulist Press (New York) and Search Press (London) put out Kasper's Christology in English under the title *Jesus the Christ*. Sometime in 1977 Collins (London) and Seabury (New York) will publish a translation of Schillebeeckx's work.

I am aware that several important themes of current Christology fail to surface in this study: for instance, the issue of method which Kasper handles so well. But I did not wish to commit the mistake of putting everything and everyone in. To list all the themes, flood the reader with names and then account for influences—both direct and indirect—of theologians on one another could only create boredom and confusion. If what is said sheds light on some major shifts which have taken place in Christology during the last twenty-five years, I will be satisfied.

I wish to express my warm thanks to Sister Michaeline O'Dwyer, R.S.H.M., for her kindness and skill in typing most of the original manuscript. The book is affectionately dedicated to all the members of my first class in the religious education program at Saint Michael's College, Winooski (Vermont).

Gerald O'Collins, S.J.

The Gregorian University
Rome
August 4, 1976.

1
Classical Christology Under Fire

Six headings gather together the major reasons for a recent swing away from the classical Christology developed by many earlier generations of theologians. It is (1) a Christology 'from above', which (2) remains incarnation-centered, (3) runs into philosophical problems, (4) mixes together historical, theological and mythical language, (5) bypasses the ministry of Jesus, and (6) separates the person of Jesus Christ from his work, that is to say, separates Christology from soteriology or the doctrine of salvation.

At once some readers may already feel uneasy with this list of reasons. What is wrong, for instance, with a Christology that 'remains incarnation-centered'? Surely the feasts of the annunciation and Christmas encourage us to see the high point of all human history as God becoming man? Yet let us at least give the reasons a hearing. Only then can we respond to them with sympathy and understanding, even if we do not leap headlong to embrace them.

(1) 'He descended from heaven' serves as the starting point for the Christology of Thomas

Aquinas, Karl Barth and other classic theologians. This Christology 'from above' bothers many of our contemporaries. They are troubled not so much by any mythological picture of a 'coming down'' from some heavenly realm. The more fundamental trouble is that this classic Christology *begins from God*. Its opening question assumes the form: How does God become man? How does the pre-existent Son of God enter our world?

This way of formulating the initial approach brings with it two difficulties. First, it has often seemed to cast doubt on the genuinely human existence of Jesus. The figure in the manger may cry like any baby. He may grow up seemingly just another boy playing on the streets of Nazareth. He may preach in the style of a wandering rabbi. The Roman forces of occupation can put him to death by that hideous combination of impalement and display which they called crucifixion. But all the same we know he is really God and this injects an element of make-believe into the whole life-story from Bethlehem on. He looks like a man, speaks like a man, suffers and dies like a man. But underneath he is divine, and this makes his genuine humanity suspect. Is he no more than God in disguise? This first difficulty with the classical Christology 'from above' runs along lines suggested by Christmas pantomimes. Daisy looks something like a cow and moos better than most cows. But all through the act we know she is no real cow at all. Right from the manger does Jesus simply play at the role of being a man?

The other difficulty about the opening question

('*How* does God become man?') arises from the answer given by the Greek Fathers of the Church to the related question 'Why?': God becomes man in order that man might become God. The possibility of imitating and sharing in the divine nature seemed easier to grasp during the early centuries of the Christian era. Today it is not simply the silence or 'felt' absence of God which makes the old theme less plausible. Man knows himself to be dehumanised in so many ways. He needs first to feel humanised before he can dream of being divinised. Man has to be 'incarnated' before he can bear to talk about the incarnation of a divine person.

(2) This brings us to the major 'mystery' in the Christology 'from above'. This kind of Christology takes *the incarnation* to be the central doctrine about Jesus Christ. Its reflections start from the nativity, not from the events of Good Friday and Easter Sunday. What happens after the incarnation becomes little more than the mere unfolding of all that has already taken place at the incarnation itself. Chalcedon encouraged this approach. The key statement from that council centered on the incarnation, and mentioned neither the crucifixion nor the resurrection.

Along with Pannenberg and other recent writers, Kasper sets his face against such an

incarnation-oriented Christology. If we allow that the divine-human person of Jesus is constituted once and for all through the incarnation, then the history and fate of Jesus—above all his cross and resurrection—have no more constitutive meaning. The death of Jesus is then merely the completion of the incarnation. The resurrection is no more than the confirmation of the divine nature.[2]

It is not that the doctrine of the incarnation should be given up. But the New Testament suggests that thinking about Jesus Christ should begin elsewhere.

St. Paul occasionally speaks of the Son's preexistence (Gal 4, 4; Rom 8, 3), but he takes the incarnation as no more than the prerequisite to the central mystery. The nativity as such neither saves us nor can it serve as the baseline for our further reflection. Paul's starting point is always Christ's saving death and resurrection. He implies that we should think of Christmas in the light of Easter, not vice versa. He offers us an elaborate list of resurrection witnesses (1 Cor 15, 5-8). But he passes over Christ's nativity in almost total silence. We hear from him no more than that Christ was born into a Jewish family (Gal 4, 4) who belonged to the house of King David (Rom 1, 3).

Paul's thinking about the sacraments ties in with his basic approach to Christ. Baptism draws believers into the crucifixion and gives them promise of resurrection (Rom 6, 3-5). We are not baptised 'into the incarnation'. The Eucharist proclaims the death of the risen Lord until he comes in glory (1 Cor 11, 26). We do not celebrate the Eucharist to proclaim the birth of Christ until he grows to manhood.

Paul's letters written from the late 40s to the early 60s made him our earliest New Testament author. When he composed his gospel around 65, St. Mark began with the baptism of Christ and left us a work which has been often described as a passion story with a long introduction. Good Friday and Easter Sunday brood over this gospel which included no nativity or incarnation stories. When they wrote later with Mark's gospel in front of them, Matthew and Luke decided to start with stories of Jesus' birth and childhood. Finally, St. John towards the close of the first century began his gospel with the sublime proclamation: 'The Word became flesh and dwelt amongst us, and we saw his glory, the glory of the only-begotten Son of the Father' (1, 14). The movement from Paul through the first three gospels to John represented an increasing concern to clarify Jesus' origins. This movement continued beyond the age of the apostles. The early centuries of controversy about Christ's identity culminated in Chalcedon's confession that Christ was one person in two natures.

If we wish to make some progress in our own wrestling with the mystery of Christ, we need to follow for ourselves the direction in which Christian thinking originally went. We must begin with the Easter Jesus, not with the Christmas Jesus. The classical Christology involves an unworkable, as well as an unbiblical, plan of attack. It reflects on what Christ was from the beginning rather than on what he did at the end. This condemns it to tortured and frustrating attempts to relate Christ's humanity and divinity within one personal existence. That brings us to the third major problem with the classical approach.

(3) By starting from the Chalcedonian confession, classical Christology instantly commits itself to endless wrestling with the questions: What terms— be they strictly or only loosely *philosophical*—should we use to relate in a true unity the being human and the being divine in Christ? How can we state the double reality of 'true God and true man', so that one aspect does not prevail at the expense of the other? This way into Christology sows dragons' teeth which instantly spring up as fully-armed problems to block our way forward.

First, *either* (a) the being human and the being divine co-exist in a dubious unity, *or* else (b) a credible humanity gets edged out for the sake of insisting on Christ's divinity. The first alternative fails to match the very council to which appeal is made. Chalcedon's confession dwells insistently on the oneness of Christ's person. In an almost literal sense, its first and last words about Jesus Christ are that he is one.

Alternative (b) has been adopted in practice by most theologians, tolerated by Church leaders and believed by vast numbers of the faithful. As Erik Routley remarks, 'traditionally an over-emphasis on the humanity has always tended to lead to positions that the church labelled as eccentric; an over-emphasis on the divinity has led to positions which were comfortably accommodated within orthodoxy.'[3] Nevertheless, such an imbalance plays false to Chalcedon itself and the pope who loomed over the council. Leo the Great insisted: 'It is as dangerous an evil to deny the truth of the human nature in Christ as to refuse to believe that his glory is equal to that of the Father' (Sermon 27, 1).

Second, Chalcedon introduced terminology from (popular) Greek philosophy in speaking of 'one person in two natures'. Of course, it neither intended to replace the New Testament message by such terminology, nor set out to define exactly what the divine nature and the human nature are. Nevertheless, the two terms (nature and person) can leave us smothered with difficulties.

Take the *two-natures* teaching. Only too easily it can suggest a Christ divided into a divine and a human layer—a double being with two natures juxtaposed. 'One person in two natures' sounds almost like a man in two jobs or someone with dual nationality. The terminology obscures the dramatic difference between being human and being divine. The 'job' of being divine is radically other than the 'job' of being human. Divine 'nationality' is worlds away from human 'nationality'.

It costs little time to ferret out the difficulties that cluster around 'person'. Even though Chalcedon did *not* call Christ a 'divine person', traditional theology has interpreted its confession in that sense. Christ is not a human person, but a divine person who assumed human nature without assuming human personality. But, as Schoonenberg argues, can Christ be completely human if he is not a human person? To deny his human personhood seems tantamount to denying that he is man. Moreover, nothing can be done to conceal the real shift between the ancient and modern concepts of 'person'. Classical theology spoke of a rational being existing in its own right. It failed to express interpersonal relations in its account, 'an individual substance of a rational nature *(naturae rationalis individua substantia)*'. Modern thought latches onto self-awareness, freedom and —in a particular way—intersubjectivity as key characteristics of a personhood. We become persons in dealing with other persons, sharing a common language and experiencing a common history. Human persons exist only in the plural. We repeat the traditional word ('person') at our peril. It has changed its meaning.[4]

(4) The fourth way in which traditional Christology has looked inadequate concerns its easy acceptance of that mixture of history, faith and mythical imagery which the old creeds present. The statements run, one after the other, as follows:

Christ was conceived by the Holy Ghost,
born of the Virgin Mary,
suffered under Pontius Pilate,
was crucified, dead and buried;
he descended into hell;
he rose again from the dead;
he ascended into heaven.

The simple listing together of these items can conceal the fact that we are constantly shifting from one order to another. Where does 'ordinary' history

begin and end? It is no surrender to nervous tren-
diness to point out that the crucifixion belongs to the
order of public history, whereas an ascension into
heaven does not. To accept that Jesus was born of
Mary and suffered under Pontius Pilate does not
demand Christian faith. But only a believer will
admit that Jesus was conceived by the Holy Ghost.

Küng reminds his readers that Christ's resurrection may not be presumed to be of the same order as
the virginal conception, the descent into hell and the
ascension, simply because the Apostles' Creed takes
all these articles of faith together. He points out that
'the oldest New Testament witness, the apostle Paul,
says nothing about virgin birth, descent into hell and
ascension. But with inexorable decisiveness he takes
the resurrection of the Crucified One as the centre of
Christian preaching.'[5]

(5) The fifth objection deals with a startling
omission in much traditional Christology. Like the
Apostles' Creed that Christology jumps straight
from 'born of the Virgin Mary' to 'suffered under
Pontius Pilate'. It undermines its usefulness by simply bypassing the history of Jesus' ministry.

Thomas Aquinas and other medieval theologians attended to the 'mysteries' of Christ's life. But
in recent centuries Christology became impoverished
by losing its capacity to think about the great features of the ministry. Even such a recent and innova-
tive work as Pannenberg's *Jesus—God and Man*
(1964) disconcertingly ignored the miracles and
other prominent themes of Jesus' life. Pannenberg
dwelt on the claims to authority, but showed no in-

terest in providing some 'personality profile' of Jesus. Moltmann's *Theology of Hope* (1964) passed over the ministry in almost total silence. Despite that book's sharp polemic against Rudolf Bultmann, it did not effectively part ways with his reduction to a minimum of the theological importance of Jesus' history. As a classical spokesman for such an approach, Kierkegaard long ago expressed the conviction that Christology need find nothing very urgent or interesting to say about the historical existence of Jesus: 'If the contemporary generation [of Jesus] had left nothing behind them but these words: "We have believed that in such and such a year God appeared among us in the humble figure of a servant, that he lived and taught in our community, and finally died," it would be more than enough.'[6]

Kasper, Küng, Schillebeeckx, Moltmann in his *The Crucified God* (1972) and other recent authors include lengthy sections on the history of Jesus. What we witness here is not a determination on the part of theologians to appear absolutely up with the latest results coming in from their colleagues engaged in purely biblical studies. Rather they refuse to take their cue from the ancient creeds of the Church and leap straight from the incarnation to the passion. What should have been obvious has come as a grand discovery. The ministry must claim attention in any serious study of Jesus Christ.

(6) Finally, much theology that took its inspiration from Chalcedon managed to separate Christology from soteriology, and felt happy to consider the person of Christ apart from his saving 'work'.

To be sure, the ancient creeds of the Church confessed the cause of Christ's 'descent from heaven' to be 'for us men and for our salvation'. Moreover, the historical setting of Chalcedon makes it clear that a deep concern for redemption lay behind the discussions of Christ's divine and human nature. The long struggle to defend and clarify his status as 'true God and true man' aimed at preserving the reality of salvation. Any tampering with either component was understood to undermine the experienced truth of redemption. If Jesus were not truly God, he would not have liberated us to share in the divine life. If he were not truly man, he would not have taken hold of and saved human life in all its fullness.

Nevertheless, the Chalcedonian teaching on the two natures seemingly 'represents Christ to us merely as an object of knowledge'. 'Such a view', Schoonenberg continues, 'detaches Christology from soteriology. This objection holds for many christological treatises which, as formal elaborations of the *unio hypostatica,* are completely distinct from soteriology.'[7] Too often Christology simply lapsed into a mass of abstract and cliché-burdened teachings about the divine-human constitution of Christ. It simply slipped out of view that not just 'Saviour' but all the other titles used of Jesus in the New Testament express aspirations for salvation. It was likewise forgotten that behind the Christological statements of the early Church we find soteriological themes. Today, however, few would disagree with Kasper's insistence that we need to overcome this separation between the person and work, between what Jesus is in himself *(in se)* and what he is for us *(pro nobis)*, between the so-called ontological and a functional approach. *How* Kasper's ideal is to be realized is another question, to which we return in the third chapter.

2
New Christological Themes

Thus far we have glanced quickly at certain features of traditional Christology which no longer win acquiescence from modern theologians. Inevitably such a rapid survey does less than justice to some aspects of the past. It is only too easy to caricature our theological forefathers and win merely pyrrhic victories over straw men. Granted, however, that some of the criticisms stick, what does the best current writing about Jesus Christ offer as a replacement? Here, as elsewhere, there is little point in exchanging one inadequate situation for another. Let us then examine what fresh lines of attack have emerged in contemporary Christology.

(1) Almost all contemporary thinking about Jesus Christ begins not 'from above' but 'from below'. It takes as its starting point (a) man, (b) the created cosmos, (c) history, or (d) some combination of all three elements. Its initial questions assume the form: What does it mean to say that a particular man was and is both universal Saviour and God-among-us? How could a man be such and be recognizable as such?

Where this Christology 'from below' chooses (a) for its way in, it may follow Küng's lead and study the experience, ideologies and faiths of human beings in the late twentieth century before going on to consider what the gospels indicate about the earthly existence of Jesus.[8] Or a Christology 'from below' may simply go straight to the humanity of Jesus. In both cases some anthropology or doctrine of man will shape the discussion. Catholic theologians may support their approach by pointing to *Gaudium et Spes* and other documents which made Vatican II the first Church council ever to deal explicitly with anthropological issues before going on to strictly theological matters. Protestant theologians may complement or introduce their Christological reflections with studies entitled *Man* (Moltmann) or *What Is Man?* (Pannenberg). It requires no special enlightenment to read off a common concern on both sides of the denominational divide. Scholars share the conviction that we can find and fashion ways of understanding Jesus, only if we attentively re-evaluate the nature of humanity itself. Christology is not proving oddly different here. An orientation towards man characterizes all the branches of contemporary theology.

Nowadays the idea that man is a changing and developing being surfaces right across the whole spectrum of human studies and theories. The process philosophy of Alfred North Whitehead, various Marxist ideologies, evolutionary humanism and all kinds of theses that stress the dynamic element in man agree at least in this. Man is a being on the way rather than a finished product, a future-oriented being who ceaselessly moves beyond himself rather than a completed essence fixed once and for all. It is against the background of such dynamic views that we now call Jesus 'true man'.

Christology 'from below' takes place in a world of thought that has been led in new directions by Darwin, Marx, Freud, Durkheim, John Stuart Mill and a host of other pioneers. The human sciences have taught us all to appreciate man in his many-faceted sociological, psychological and political dimensions. Theologians can hardly be expected to forget all this schooling once they turn to consider Jesus of Nazareth. It would be schizoid to inhabit one world as a result of one's seminary training and another world as a result of one's university studies.

Duquoc introduces sociological interpretation and psychoanalytic theories in his two-volume work, *Christologie, essai dogmatique.*[9] Whatever our verdict on the merits of this particular Christology 'from below', it exemplifies the need not only to recognise and affirm in Jesus the fullness of human existence, but also to do that in a world of thought shaped by the human sciences. Once we agree that as a genuine human being Jesus developed psychologically, we cannot then ignore Freud, Jung and Erikson by refusing even to raise the question: What could that development have been like—before and after puberty?

Instead of, or as well as, starting from considerations about (a) human existence a Christology 'from below' may choose to begin from (b) the whole created *cosmos* or (c) from the *history* of the world. (b) Teilhard de Chardin interpreted the appearance of Christ within his scheme of evolutionary optimism. As the whole of creation moved dynamically forward and upward, Christ marked a unique leap from the lower level of matter towards a higher spiritual unity. (c) History plays a large role in the Christologies 'from below' developed by Moltmann and Pannenberg. In taking the crucified Jesus as the origin of all Christian theology, Moltmann develops a Christology situated 'after Auschwitz' and within the whole *history of suffering*. Pannenberg endorses the Hegelian principle that the truth is in the whole. Universal history becomes the place to look when we seek the truth about Jesus of Nazareth. His resurrection anticipates the end of world history and allows us to find in his destiny the revelation of God. History—whether the history of suffering, universal history or some other version of history—can offer perspectives from which to organize the material taken into one's Christology.

Whichever precise way it runs, a Christology 'from below' will probably safeguard the genuine human existence of Jesus. But will it compel us to push beyond his created humanity and confess, 'My Lord and my God'? What was so special about him when set over against the great prophets, the martyred Socrates or the finest among the ancient rabbis? Classical Christology 'from above' could quickly lay its finger on the distinctive element. The Word of God was incarnate in Jesus the man. Current Christology 'from below', however, may point to the supreme love shown by Jesus, his 'being for others', his sinlessness, or his being 'the unique, *supreme*, case of the total actualization of human reality'.[10] 'Face' has become a favorite word to express the special factor. Küng speaks of 'God with the face of Jesus'.[11] John Robinson chose *The Human Face of God* as the title for his Christology, and Schillebeeckx sums up his conclusions as follows: 'The person of Jesus is the revelation of the eschatological face of all humanity and in that the revelation of the trinitarian plenitude of the unique God as absolutely free gift to man.'[12]

Any of these Christologies 'from below' crashes into a perennial problem here. Do they say enough to justify us calling Jesus 'true man *and true God*'? Mere sinlessness or being 'the man for others' fails to take us that far. Likewise, the supreme divine revelation could take place through the person of Jesus without our needing to agree that in looking on his face we are literally looking on the face of God. The agent of divine revelation cannot automatically be assumed to be identical with God.

Debates between Christologies 'from above' and Christologies 'from below' can leave us fretting over charges and counter-charges about pastoral responsibility, fidelity to Chalcedon and the rest. Last year—to my discredit—I found myself participating in such polemics. A conservative theologian hit out at Küng: 'He is driving people out of the Church by not stating clearly that Christ was and is God.' I struck back: 'Others have driven people out of the Church by not stating clearly that Christ was and is man.'

Both Christologies have their difficulties. On balance, however, most contemporary theologians prefer to attempt a Christology 'from below' and practise Augustine's principle, 'Through the man Christ you move to the God Christ' (Sermon 261, 7).

(2) Unlike theologians of the past, most practitioners of Christology 'from below' centre on the *death and resurrection*. Not all, however. Karl Rahner describes the incarnation as the 'climax' in 'the total history of the human race'. In his view, the death and resurrection of Christ, being already 'implied and accepted' at the outset, turn out to be an unfolding of 'the absolute mystery of the incarnation'.[13] Others like John Robinson in effect make evolving creation itself the primary focus. He insists that Jesus was, 'with the rest of us, a genuine product of the evolutionary process'. The stardust at the foundation of the world prepared the way for the coming of Jesus.[14] Here one detects, peeping over Robinson's shoulder, the looming figure of Teilhard. The bishop's *Human Face of God* includes some remarks on Jesus' resurrection, but bypasses Calvary to the point that neither 'cross' nor 'crucifixion' appears in the index. The book makes nothing of the fact that the human face of God became disfigured and silent at Calvary.

Where Rahner and Robinson focus—respectively—on the incarnation and creation, others like Küng revert to the ministry of Jesus as the heart of the matter. It is not that Küng neglects to discuss the events of Good Friday and Easter Sunday. But he seems most at home with Jesus' activity as preacher and healer. With deep and serious feeling he analyses the Sermon on the Mount, the new commandment of love, the miracles and other gospel themes which offer the clearest possible picture of Jesus as he actually lived and impressed himself on his hearers.

Given that we have no decisive consensus, does it really matter where a Christology 'from below' finds its central focus? Why not latch onto creation, the incarnation, the ministry or even the final coming of Christ? Such a tolerant pluralism will not work, at least not if we wish to share the central New Testament approach. The first Christians knew themselves to be healed and graced as a result of those days when the Lord 'was put to death for our trespasses and raised for our justification' (Rom 4, 25). Through faith and baptism they enjoyed the power which flowed from the paschal mystery. They were not 'baptised into' the creation, the ministry of Jesus or his final coming. Not that they devalued these further aspects of their total belief. But they found in the resurrection of their crucified Lord the centre from which they looked forward and backward to the other mysteries of faith.

(3) Earlier we noted some difficulties that confront classical Christology in its use of language and philosophical terminology. Any Christology from below would only be bluffing if it pretended to avoid all such terminology and its attendant difficulties. Kasper rightly requires that every Christology must be properly philosophical. Any serious discussion of Jesus Christ brings us into the deep water where we confront the final meaning of reality and the most basic needs of man. An undertow of philosophical issues tugs at Christology from start to finish. The

ultimate and universal quality of the questions raised by the life, death and resurrection of Jesus demands that we accept help from philosophers. We cannot satisfy this demand by using sociology and other human sciences. If we remove philosophy at one point, we will find it coming back at another.

Schillebeeckx and Schoonenberg exemplify the way philosophical questions inevitably surface in any worthwhile account of Jesus Christ. A sentence from Schillebeeckx was quoted above: 'The person of Jesus is the revelation of the eschatological face of all humanity.' Obviously we move straight into philosophical discussion, once we ask for the meaning of 'person', 'revelation' and 'humanity'. And what counts as an 'eschatological face'? Schoonenberg argues for a Christology of 'presence'. Philosophy necessarily intrudes once we start to question the nature of this presence. Are we dealing with the mutual presence of passengers on a rush-hour bus? Or the presence of parents with their children? Or some presence of God experienced by those gathered for worship? As soon as we seek to sort out just what these and other kinds of presence ultimately entail, we move into genuinely philosophical analysis.

In the past, Greek philosophy, both directly or more often in a diluted form, helped theological musings and at times even held them together. Some theologians may have refused to espouse Aristotle's five causes, doctrines about 'prime matter' and reflections on 'substance and accidents'. Nevertheless, to a degree all shared in the one perennial philosophy deriving ultimately from the Greeks. In the last century or so things have fallen apart, even if much debris from that perennial philosophy still lies around.

A new philosophical pluralism affects Christology no less than any other branch of theology. Schillebeeckx mixes Thomism, existentialism and some elements from linguistic philosophy. Boff draws on Marxist and Teilhardian themes. Hegelian terminology pops up everywhere in Kasper's *Jesus der Christus* to betray his heritage from German idealism.

What forces itself on our attention here is the constant need for philosophical awareness. At times traditional Christology used debased philosophical language which was hideous and empty of meaning. Contemporary Christology can fail in stringency and coherence. Küng's *Christ sein* serves to illustrate this.

Küng rightly draws attention to the rich variety of ways in which piety, literature, theology, art and Church teaching have represented Christ. He asks: 'Which is the true picture of Christ?' He then introduces a give-away comparison: 'Too many different and possibly touched-up photographs of one and the same person can make detective work difficult. And detective work—often one of the most exciting and tense efforts at discovery—is again and again a really considerable part of Christian theology.'[15] He presses on to offer a long discussion entitled 'The Real Christ'.[16] He warns us to be ready for surprises as we join him in the task of detection and look for 'the original Jesus'.[17]

Three things make Küng's method suspect. First, he seems to presuppose that some *one* picture or description will give us the true Jesus. This premise ignores the fact that, in describing persons, indefinitely many true accounts are possible. It would be nonsense to line up all Rembrandt's self-portraits and after a careful comparison select one as the only true picture of the artist. Are we to scrutinize all the literature about Napoleon on the supposition that we can finally hold up just one biography and declare, 'That's the real Napoleon'? Various portraits, accounts and biographical reflections can all be describing the same person truly. Some say more and others less. We will expect a number of common pictures. But we may not compare and contrast them on the grounds that only one will turn out to be *the* genuine 'photograph' of the person in question.

Second, I am not convinced that Küng sufficiently alerts his readers to the irreducible difference between (a) Jesus Christ *in himself* and (b) *any* picture, idea or description Küng and others may have *of him*. We can use the gospels, traditional faith and practice, and our own experience to check and correct our description of Jesus. But we may never reduce 'the real Christ' even to our most carefully formed and cherished picture of him.

Third, analogies should not, of course, be expected to indicate all that is involved. Nevertheless, the comparison with detective work risks implying that our study of Jesus and his history can be pressed into the mould of some neutral science of detection. Not only in the case of Jesus but in the study of history generally the past becomes present only as something conditioned by one's personal attitudes. My set of beliefs must inevitably colour any interpretation of Karl Marx, Oliver Cromwell or Abraham Lincoln. Both Küng's comparison with detective work and other material in *Christ sein* (to which we will return later) can imply a spurious objectivity in historical investigation. It is dangerous to suggest that we can act like detectives—hunting through the available materials and using some special scientific skills until we finally seize the *real* Jesus, faster and, so to speak, more objectively than others. Add, too, that perennial conviction and experience of Christians. *We* do not hunt down Jesus. He is the divine detective tracking us down. We find him because he has first found us.

(4) The fourth complaint we considered in the first section came from traditional Christology's failure to sort out history, mythical imagery and theological belief in the various doctrines about Christ listed in the Apostles' Creed. We can sample some of contemporary Christology's contributions here.

Few readers, I suspect, will be troubled by Küng's remarks on the ascension. But many will be upset by what he maintains about the virginal conception of Jesus. First, the ascension. Küng points out that the story about the risen Lord being taken up into the sky before the eyes of his followers (Acts 1, 9-11) has a double function: to mark the end of the 'ordinary' Easter appearances,[18] and to introduce the Church's mission which will last until the Lord comes again. The ascension was not in fact a separate happening in its own right, but an aspect of the total Easter-event. Luke communicates his message by means of a story.[19] Only fundamentalists will insist that forty days after the resurrection the Lord literally 'took off' for heaven from the Mount of Olives and then two angels came to send the disciples home to Jerusalem.

On the virginal conception Küng draws attention to the silence of Mark, Paul and John. They proclaim Jesus as Son of God, without ever mentioning the virginal conception. They believe that the appearance of Jesus meant a startlingly new situation for mankind and the world. But accepting this today, Küng suggests, may not be made easier by 'the legend' of a miraculous conception. 'No one', he argues, 'can be obliged to believe in the biological fact of a virginal conception.'[20]

If many Catholics will find this position helpful and liberating, others will angrily part ways with Küng here: 'Having demythologized papal infallibility, he now turns on the Virgin Mary. Where will it all stop?' Ultimately, however, any discussion can settle down and become fruitful only if we agree to change our fundamental question from '*Where* will it all stop?' to '*How* do we stop?' *How* should we go about interpreting the scriptures and traditional belief on this or that point? What principles should we apply in this task of 'faith seeking understanding'?

Any serious reflection on the virginal conception would mean indulging an enormous parenthesis. Interested readers might consult Raymond Brown's valuable treatment.[21] I must, however, confess some

misgivings about Brown's language and presuppositions. At the end of a careful and reasonable look at
material from scripture, traditional teaching and theology, Brown sums up: 'My judgment, in conclusion,
is that the totality of the *scientifically controllable*
evidence leaves an unresolved problem—a conclusion that should not disappoint since I used the word
"problem" in my title.'[22] But do the connotations of
the word 'problem' somewhat prejudice matters
right from the outset? In handling such doctrines as
Christ's virginal conception, resurrection, ascension
and presence in the Eucharist, we do not engage in
problem-solving but enter the area of mystery. To be
sure, a rational investigation of Church tradition and
good exegesis of the New Testament texts are necessary, but they are not sufficient. Will 'scientifically
controllable' evidence alone ever prove decisive as
regards, let us say, Christ's presence in the Eucharist? What would count as evidence here? What
kind of science stands behind the words 'scientifically controllable'? Perhaps I am being unduly
fussy. Yet, granted that it would be wrong to take
Christ's resurrection as 'a problem' to be discussed
on the basis of 'the totality of the scientifically controllable evidence', what allows us to approach the
virginal conception in that way?[23]

(5) Recently theologians have remedied their
predecessors' neglect by introducing material from
Jesus' ministry as essential for any adequate Christology. But, to put it mildly, the ministry of Jesus is no
simple, easily grasped phenomenon. Three themes
can be singled out for particular attention: (a) the

Christology implicit in the ministry, (b) Jesus as the 'principle' for criticizing the Church, and (c) his language as a key to his imagination.

(a) For fifty years or more debates have raged about Jesus' sense of his personal identity. Did he know himself to be *and* call himself Messiah, Son of God, Son of Man and Suffering Servant? If so, what meaning did he attach to those notions in evaluating and revealing himself? At times these debates moved from the historical record, as far as it is recoverable, to the area of principle. *Could* Jesus have *been* Son of God and Messiah without knowing that clearly or at least without in some way being aware of that? Is such a separation between the order of *being* (his actual identity) and the order of *knowledge* (his self-awareness) tolerable and plausible?

Bruce Vawter, for instance, blends history and principle to make his point in this debate:

To say that Jesus in his earthly life knew and judged himself to be God's natural Son and very God is to assert the *unprovable* and, from the perspective of the New Testament, the improbable. Had Jesus known such a thing he *could hardly* have contained his knowledge, yet the gospels are witness that his most intimate disciples did not recognize his essential relation to God prior to the resurrection.[24]

We can unpack the argument. Even if X (Jesus'

knowing and judging 'himself to be God's natural Son and very God') were the case, we could never prove it. Besides if X were the case, then Y: Jesus 'could hardly' have kept this to himself. But we have no evidence that he ever blurted out this secret. Therefore, X was not the case. The real issue here, of course, touches Vawter's theological and/or philosophical grounds for claiming that X is 'unprovable', and that, if X, then Y 'could hardly' have failed to take place. Such argumentation has obviously shifted out of the field of 'mere' exegesis.

Many exegetes, however, have been content to subject certain texts to repeated and minute scrutiny. Did Jesus really say 'The Son of Man also came not to be served but to serve, and to give his life as a ransom for many' (Mk 10, 45)? If these were in fact his words, was he consciously identifying himself as both the Son of Man (Dan 7, 13f.) and the Suffering Servant of Isaiah? Did he mean to distinguish himself from the Son of Man in glory? Or take that 'Johannine meteorite fallen on the Synoptic earth', a saying that at first glance suggests the 'high' doctrine of divine Sonship one finds in the fourth gospel: 'No one knows the Son except the Father, and no one knows the Father except the Son and anyone to whom the Son chooses to reveal him' (Mt 11, 27). Does this verse not only come from Jesus himself, but also imply an uniquely exclusive way of being God's Son?

Such discussions moved in one way or another around the topic of Christological *titles*, their meaning and their use or non-use by Jesus and his contemporaries. Some scholars like Geza Vermes in *Jesus the Jew* continue to keep the issue of titles alive. This study leads to the conclusion that Jesus' intimates and even his less committed admirers venerated him as Prophet, Lord and Son of God.

Recently, however, more stress has been laid on the *general attitudes* of Jesus as a key to the way he identified himself. Thus Küng refuses to begin by examining the titles which might 'go back' to the ministry of Jesus. We will only get into a mess if our arguments for Jesus' self-understanding rest on a debatable conclusion about some one title or particular verse. Apologists have made much, for instance, of the interchange between Jesus and the high priest during the trial. Yet they had to establish that Jesus replied to the question 'Are you the Christ, the Son of God' (Mt 26, 64) with a straight 'I am' (Mk 14, 62). His answer did not take a noncommittal form, 'The words are yours' (Mt 26, 64). Moreover, apologists needed to prove that somehow the disciples had access to the trial proceedings and faithfully reported the master's self-description on that occasion. Rather than get trapped in such debates, Küng points rather to the broad and undeniable characteristics of the ministry.[25]

The preaching of Jesus implied a stunning claim to authority. At times he called the Mosaic law into question, put himself above that law and spoke in God's place. A willingness to lose his life and act as the servant of all drove him to associate with tax agents, prostitutes and further groups considered undesirable by the 'good' people. To all he expressed the divine pardon and love. By eating with people who were obviously and openly guilty, he received them into God's company. Jesus' claim was clear. Deciding for or against him became tantamount to deciding for or against the divine rule itself.

What earthly Jesus *implied* about himself unfolded in the light of the crucifixion and resurrection into the full-blown Christology of the post-Easter Church. It was *not* a movement from a low to a high Christology, as if Jesus made only minimal and modest claims about his personal identity which were later maximized into the high Christology which called him Lord, Son of God and—eventually —God. Rather the shift took place between the implicit Christology of the ministry and the explicit Christology of the emerging Church. Many scholars of all denominations make such an implied Christology one of their major conclusions from a study of Jesus' ministry.

(b) Above I spoke of Jesus being used as 'a principle for criticising the Church'. This phrase masks two related but distinguishable tendencies in contemporary theology. First of all, at every level it has become clear that more and more Church leaders, theologians and other Christians have recognized that ecclesiastical issues will never be resolved unless we push further back—to our understanding of Christ himself. Christology criticizes and determines ecclesiology, but not vice versa. What we do with the Church will rest, or should rest, on what we think about Jesus.

Both during and after the Second Vatican

Council Schillebeeckx and Küng devoted their theological expertise to the cause of community reform.
With prodigal energy Küng wrote about the Church
—her past, present and future. Back in 1965 Kasper
published his *Dogma unter dem Wort Gottes*, a
book that widely influenced thinking on dogmatic
formulations. Instinctively all three theologians
swung in unison towards the basic Christological
issues and in the same year (1974) produced their
Jesus-books. The twelve years since the closing of
the Council have shown that any efforts to renew the
Church will remain spiritually empty, emotionally
hollow and doctrinally unsound unless they draw inspiration and strength from the founder of Christianity himself. The Council attended to ecclesiastical problems. It produced a range of documents on
the Church, ecumenism, the liturgy, relations with
other religions, the roles of bishops, priests, religious
and laity, missionary activity and the rest. But it
considered Christology only secondarily. If Vatican
III were to meet in late 1977, its major document
would not be 'The Church in the Modern World' but
some response to the question: Who is Jesus Christ
for us today? Vawter brought out into the open what
many were thinking by insisting on just such a
'priority of Christ' over any ecclesiastical issues.[26]

Second, the historical figure of Jesus can come
into play not simply to remind us that ecclesiastical
doctrines must be subordinated to Christological beliefs, but to provide grounds for criticising—at times
intensely—current Church life. Käsemann in his
Jesus Means Freedom and elsewhere has underlined

that unique freedom which Jesus both gave and de-
manded. And yet 'freedom', Käsemann reflects, is
one of the last words Church leaders wish to hear, let
alone use. Boff *(Jésus-Christ Libérateur)* takes the
standpoint of Latin American theology to maintain
that every theology of liberation must establish Jesus
as a critical principle *against* the Church. Holl *(Jesus
in Bad Company)* sees the challenge of Jesus' ministry in this question: Will society and the Church
come to grips with their forgotten minorities and
worry less about the 'good', average people?

Küng presses anachronistic language into service and finishes up with a Jesus whose conflicts with
Jewish leaders—dare one say it?—prefigure the author's own battles with Church authorities. *Christ
sein* repeatedly speaks of the 'Jewish hierarchy'
whose zeal for the 'prevailing dogmas' and 'infallible
propositions' brings Jesus down. The political
charges before Pilate conceal the 'envy of the hierarchy and its court-theologians'. An 'inquisitorial zeal
for the law' prevents the hierarchy from letting 'this
radical' go. He is provoking proper authority, represents 'a rebellion against the hierarchy and its theology' and would only cause 'confusion and insecuri-
ty'.[27]

How should we assess the current efforts to take
the story of Jesus as a basis for criticising the Christian Church? On the one hand, such approaches can
go wildly wrong. An interest in Jesus may be used to
justify disengagement from the Church, as if one
could truly and fully find him apart from the community he called into being. Or else talk about Jesus

and his ministry may lapse into feasting on the carri-
on comfort of abusing Church leaders.

On the other hand, however, the history of Jesus
can undoubtedly stand in judgment on the way
Christians often live and react. An anecdote from
the 1960s illustrates this point better than any argument. A Catholic curate told his bishop how he
had arranged an ecumenical service for the boys and
girls from the local high school. The arrangement
had been made that the non-Catholic students would
leave after a bible service, while the Catholics would
remain for a Mass. 'But they all stayed', the curate
explained, 'and at the time for Holy Communion
most of them started coming up to the altar.' 'What
did you do?' the bishop asked. 'Well', said the
curate, 'I thought to myself, what would Jesus have
done?' The bishop broke in aghast: 'You didn't, did
you?'

Too often, of course, neither individual Christians nor Christian communities even ask themselves: 'What would Jesus do?' Rather they invoke
his name and authority to support religious practices, social standards and political activities that
they have *already* endorsed on other grounds. Here
none of us have any conscience to examine but our
own. But we will find that few methods have greater
power to create true sensitivity towards the divine
will than regular meditation on episodes from the
ministry of Jesus. In that way his ministry can become a principle for deeply criticising our own lives.

(c) Finally, the *language* of Jesus' ministry continues to attract fresh studies. Their findings vary

enormously in value. A recent work concluded by announcing that 'Jesus emerges from this study as one whose language must be distinguished from casual speech'! Is this another example of scholars making the obvious look like a great discovery?

One approach which has been monotonously neglected but which seems worth pursuing is the language of Jesus *as a clue to his imagination*. Without presenting us with an exact transcript of the words Jesus used, the synoptic writers (Matthew, Mark and Luke) preserve the flow and flavour of his preaching. This expressive language allows us to glimpse the ways in which his imagination functioned. His eye had scanned a great deal of normal human living. His sensibility betrayed its preferences. He employed, for instance, a large number of farming images but few images drawn from history, geography, warfare and some aspects of home life, for instance the mother-child relationship. There was a hereness and a nowness about the language of Jesus, a preoccupation with the scene right in front of him. In short, the images he used yield some hints about the way he perceived his world.[28]

Let us now conclude this chapter. Our first chapter noted the tendency of traditional theology to separate the person of Christ from his saving 'work', that is to say, Christology from soteriology. This separation divided him into two zones of reality, *who* he was/is and *what* he did/does. In the next chapter we examine how well contemporary theology overcomes this division.

3
Soteriology
and Christology

The first chapter noted how classical theology normally treated the *person* of Jesus Christ apart from his saving *work*. To put this in technical terms, Christology was separated from soteriology. In this chapter we reflect on contemporary attempts to overcome the person-work separation and deal with salvation through Christ.

Functional or Ontological?

When they seek to rehabilitate soteriology, many of the wiser spirits today remark that they do *not* intend to choose a merely functional approach and abandon ontological assertions about Jesus. Kasper dismisses any such 'dilemma' of 'an ontological and a functional Christology' as 'a fictitious problem and an alternative into which theology should not let itself get maneuvered'.[29] Jesus' value and function for us demand that we examine and recognize his status at the level of his being. His saving work indicates both *who* he was and is—both in himself and in his relationship to the Father. There can be no satisfactory account of what Jesus does if we dismiss as unimportant the question who he is. Every soteriological statement has its Christological implications. This point has won wide acceptance and in any case seems obvious enough. To go on insisting that one cannot pursue a functional approach without somehow taking an ontological stand looks like exhuming and beating a thoroughly dead horse.

Nevertheless, some critics of Küng's *Christ sein* level the charge that, when he finally comes to discuss Christ's pre-existence, he lapses into a merely functional Christology. The book may offer an unsatisfactory version of pre-existence. But my point here is this. In principle it appears impossible to speak of some person's value, significance and role without making at least some implicit claims about the nature of that person. A merely functional Christology which sets aside ontological issues is simply not feasible. Küng declines to try his hand at such an impossible task. His approach may be 'primarily' functional, but it is not exclusively so.[30]

From Implicit to Explicit Soteriology

Genuine debate has flared up in recent years over the redemptive value that Jesus attached to his coming death. Theoretically, two extremes are possible here. (a) One the one hand, it could be argued that there was no connection at all between what Jesus intended and what actually overtook him. Crucifixion abruptly cut his life short and brought salvation to the human race. But he neither expected nor intended to bring this about. The value of his death in no sense derived from his deliberate purposes. (b) On the other hand, one might assert that Calvary and its effects were totally foreseen by Jesus—right from babyhood. Past versions of that extreme account described his death as premeditated to the extent that they made it look like suicide. Or at any rate his life became cruelly incredible. It was spent under a conscious countdown to death by torture killing. What sense could we make of a man who right from his cradle clearly anticipated and fully accepted a crucifixion which he knew to be fixed for a certain day, hour and place?

Among recent writers Pannenberg has gone as far as any in playing down the voluntary obedience of Jesus. The way he explains matters, Jesus was so seized by his mission that he was scarcely left with any genuinely human choice about accepting or refusing his fate on Calvary.[31] At the other end of the spectrum of opinions, Muggeridge attributes to Jesus a long-range knowledge and acceptance of his execution. Jesus realized from the start that something dreadful waited for him at the end of the road. Yet even Muggeridge pulls back from suggesting that right from the beginning Jesus anticipated and accepted death in the precise form of crucifixion. He writes: 'From the beginning, it had been borne in upon him that the only possible outcome of the mission on earth God had confided to him was an ignominious and *public death*.'[32]

All in all, it is hard to find any contemporary author, whether scholarly or popular, settling clearly for either of the extremes mentioned above. Nevertheless, a recent debate (in German) between Hans Kessler, Heinz Schürmann and others exemplifies the trend either to minimalize or maximalize matters. Kessler has pressed the case that the crucifixion was something which overtook Jesus rather than being a destiny which he embraced and interpreted in advance. Schürmann, however, insists that Jesus understood his coming death as the culmination of his mission and—within the circle of his disciples—used his farewell meal to indicate that human salvation would result from his execution.[33]

Any discussion here will only shamble and shuffle along if it fails to distinguish between ascertainable facts and intelligible principles—or, if you like, between historical exegesis and theology. A passage from Vawter's *This Man Jesus* illustrates the way in which an argument can shift from the historical to the theological level:

Did he [i.e., Jesus] not only foresee his death as a substantive part of his mission, but also cast himself in a role like that of the Servant of the Lord . . .? It is probably impossible to prove either that he did or did not. . . . The fact that has validated belief in the atoning power of Jesus' death is not the psychology of Jesus, but the atonement itself. . . . The testimony of Christian men who professed their lives to be

God's gift through a crucified Saviour thus established the "fact" of vicarious atonement in a way that Jesus' premonition of it *could* [not] or *did* not.[34]

The case here moves from (a) what historians may establish concerning the things Jesus 'foresaw'—his 'psychology' and 'premonitions' about his execution—to (b) what 'could' validate and establish the redemptive value of that death.

To my mind, no version of Calvary delivers a satisfactory form of *theological* goods unless it appreciates how Jesus went knowingly and willingly to his death. If we strike out any genuinely free purpose on his part, we turn him into a passive victim whose murder God picked to serve for the salvation of mankind. Such a version certainly cannot enlist support from the contemporary readiness to recognize how far personal freedom shapes reality. In an essential way subjective intentions affect the meaning of actions. We can only expect that the value of Good Friday was deeply determined by Jesus' own free decision, no less than by the deliberate choices of other men and the freely adopted divine strategy for human salvation. Here one might parody an old principle and say: *Extra libertatem Christi nulla salus*. Theologians should know better than to interpret Calvary in terms of the Father's freedom and our freedom, while making little of Jesus' freedom in consciously dying for certain purposes. Once we acknowledge how much the voluntary quality of the crucifixion matters, we must press on and ask: What did Jesus hope to achieve through his martyrdom? Thus our theological anxiety to respect his freedom brings us to scrutinize the historical evidence.

Here Schürmann and other scholars admit that in trying to recapture Jesus' intentions in the face of death, we may feel we are largely pulling at broken strings. In Mark 10, 45 Jesus seemingly identified himself with the 'Suffering Servant' whose death would atone for human sin: 'The Son of Man came not to be served but to serve, and to give his life as a ransom for many.' But can we treat this verse as reporting the *ipsissima verba*? In particular, do the words 'a ransom for many' come from the historical Jesus himself? The story of the Last Supper prom-ises that the crucifixion will mediate a new covenant between God and the human race: 'This is my blood of the covenant, which is poured out for many' (Mk 14, 24). But how far has the Eucharistic liturgy of the early Church modified what Jesus actually said the night before he died? The doubts raised about these and other texts may trouble us to the point of deciding to contract out of historical debates and set-tle for some 'safe' view—a theology which leaves aside the intentions of Jesus before his death. How-ever, we need not despair and in this way abandon history for theology. If the *ipsissima verba* of Jesus often elude us, we can be confident of pinning down something of his *ipsissima intentio*.[35]

Violent death was much more than a vague pos-sibility for Jesus. Herod Antipas killed John the Baptist, Jesus' precursor. To preserve law and order in Palestine the Romans took life easily. From some of his Jewish contemporaries Jesus ran into menacing opposition over the content of his preaching and the style of his life. He relativised sacred traditions, broke the sabbath rest to heal people, associated with religious outcasts, showed himself master in the Jerusalem Temple by temporarily assuming authority there and—in his own name—interpreted the divine will and communicated the divine pardon. Doubtless the gospels exaggerate the extent of the conflict with the Pharisees, Sadducees and other groups. But it is clear that by the end of Jesus' ministry no major religious and/or political body would step forward to defend him. When he made his journey to Jerusalem and cleansed the Temple, the situation could only have looked extremely threatening. Most readers will find little difficulty in agreeing that—like the prophets before him—Jesus put himself on a deadly collision course through fidelity to his vocation. We may, however, flounder and stagger when faced with the question: What did Jesus *intend to bring about* by accepting the victim-role which was thrust upon him? The evidence seems fugitive right at this decisive point.

Schürmann and others point us in the right direction. They recall attitudes which characterised the ministry of Jesus: service, love and engagement on behalf of sinners. He went about as one who wished to serve all, associated with sinners and offered them God's forgiveness—despite the outrage this caused to 'the righteous'. Geza Vermes sums up this unique feature of Jesus' practice:

In one respect more than any other he differed from both his contemporaries and even his prophetic predecessors. The prophets spoke on behalf of the honest poor, and defended the widows and the fatherless, those oppressed and exploited by the wicked, rich and powerful. Jesus went further. In addition to proclaiming these blessed, he actually took his stand among the pariahs of his world, those despised by the respectable. Sinners were his table-companions and the ostracised tax-collectors and prostitutes his friends.[36]

The consistent characteristics of Jesus' mission of love converge to suggest his *ipsissima intentio*. He anticipated and accepted death not simply as the consequence of his prophetic mission but as a last service of love. Death was the climax of a ministry during which, as Schillebeeckx insists, *every* action announced, promised and offered salvation.[37]

In these terms the whole ministry yields one major clue to Jesus' attitudes when faced with his violent death. The other major clue comes from the current Jewish idea that a just man could represent others and expiate their sins by dying. This conviction was in the air. It would seem almost unaccountably odd that the vicarious role of his death never occurred to Jesus. He who had shown himself the Servant of all accepted the vocation to become the *Suffering* Servant for all.

These considerations prevent the redemptive

message of the Last Supper from coming as a complete surprise. Jesus knew his impending death would atone for the sins of 'many'. Moreover, he linked his fate with the coming rule of God. The liturgy of the early Church simply does not account for one key saying from the Last Supper narrative: 'Truly, I say to you, I shall not drink again of the fruit of the vine until that day when I drink it new in the kingdom of God' (Mk 14, 25). This text takes us right back to Jesus' last meal with his core-group, that 'night before he died.' In brief, the coming rule of God and atonement for sin shaped the *ipsissima intentio* of Jesus—at least during the last days of his ministry.

We can speak of the earthly Jesus' largely *implicit* soteriology which Paul and the early Church developed into an *explicit* soteriology. Brown and other scholars have talked of the implicit Christology of the ministry being succeeded by the explicit Christology of the post-Easter community.[38] This terminology which concerns the *person* of Jesus can be usefully extended to his work. Kasper prefers to contrast a 'hidden soteriology' of Jesus' ministry with the revealed soteriology proclaimed after Pentecost.[39] It seems, however, rather distracting and intrusive to vary terminology here. An implicit/explicit soteriology both matches the popular scheme of an implicit/explicit Christology, and truly expresses the shift from (a) what the preaching of Jesus implied about salvation to (b) what the Holy Spirit led Paul to affirm clearly: Christ 'gave himself for our sins to deliver us from the present evil age' (Gal 1, 4).

The Language of Salvation

Most scholars writing on Jesus Christ show
themselves sensitively aware of the need to watch
their language and not thoughtlessly slip into adopt-
ing current jargon. Did Jesus prove to be a 'revolutionary'? Is the salvation he promised usefully called
'liberation'? Or have revolution and liberation become catch-all terms applied to such a wide variety
of phenomena that soteriology can well do without
this language?

Küng takes 'revolution' to apply properly to the
sudden and violent overthrowing of some social
order. He points to the evidence against describing
Jesus as a social revolutionary. But then he comes
around to allow that Jesus proved to be 'more revolutionary than the revolutionaries'.[40] Others betray
nervousness over 'liberation'. Its political connotations may misrepresent the saving message of Jesus.
Kasper knows the problems, but he keeps his head,
recalls the concern with 'emancipation' that sprang
from the Enlightenment,[41] and ends by presenting
redemption as 'liberation *(Befreiung)*'.[42]

It would be unfair to belittle the performance of
any theologians as they wrestle with the terminology
to be used about salvation. Nevertheless, some show
themselves heedless of the niceties of language when
it comes to dealing with one topic—Christ's precise
role. Words like 'representative *(Stellvertreter)*',
'substitute *(Ersatzmann)*' and 'solidarity' continue to
be employed in a confused and cumbersome way.

A decade ago critics took issue with Pannenberg
for the carelessness he showed in explaining how

Christ was our 'penal substitute'. If someone genuinely represents me, I must agree to his doing so and
he must freely undertake the task. Representation is
voluntary on both sides, as well as being restricted to
specific areas and limited periods of time. A substitute, however, may be simply put in the place of
another person or thing. Thus we can substitute a
pawn for a castle on a chess-board. Another football
player may serve as substitute for a player injured on
his way to a match. On the field the substitute takes
the place of the injured man, who may be uncon-
scious and hence without knowledge that someone is
acting as his substitute. In wartime another prisoner
may be shot in place of one who has escaped. There
should be no need to pile up further examples to
illustrate the point. In the case of substitution between persons, the parties concerned may neither
know nor be willing that the substitution is taking
place. There is less intentionality and more passivity
apparent in the way we use the language of 'substitution'. This consideration alone should win support
for speaking of 'Christ our representative' and not of
'Christ our substitute'.

Küng does not take the necessary care about
terminology in this area. He moves easily from talk-
ing about Christ's *solidarity* and identification with
'sinners of all kinds' to conclude that 'he died as the
sinners' representative'—indeed, as mankind's *representative* 'before God'.[43] But what counts as representation here? I can feel deep solidarity with a
group of suffering people without being their representative. Conversely, someone can have power of

attorney for me, although I feel little solidarity with this legal representative. Küng's usage may not win acquiescence from those schooled to be precise in language.

Kasper also should be more discriminating about such words as 'representative', 'discipleship' and 'solidarity'. He argues that Jesus' 'call to discipleship . . . implied the notion of representation'.[44] This seems wide of the mark. Some 'master' can invite me to be his disciple without undertaking to be my representative before God and man. No one that I have met considers himself to be a disciple of his legal representative, although some people take that attitude toward their political representatives. In general, discipleship and representation do not necessarily imply each other. Doubtless the disciples of Jesus enjoyed a degree of solidarity with the master who invited them to follow him. One can also admit that it belonged to this discipleship that he did 'something "for us" '.[45] But more evidence is required to show that *as such* 'the call to discipleship'—at least in the case of Jesus—implied 'the notion of representation'. He said to Simon and Andrew: 'Follow me and I will make you become fishers of men' (Mk 1, 17). The call to discipleship did not take the form of saying or implying: 'Follow me and I will become your saving representative before my Father in dying to expiate your sins'. When the language of expiation surfaces later, Mark has Jesus speak of giving his life 'as a ransom for many' (10, 45), and not just as a ransom for the disciples with him. Of course, one might simply identify Jesus' disciples with all those saved through his representative death and resurrection. In that case the call to discipleship would coincide with a call to salvation as such and hence imply representation. The commission to 'make disciples of all nations' (Mt 28, 19) could encourage us to adopt this broad notion of discipleship. But in that case we must cease thinking of discipleship as entailing some special generosity which only a small minority can muster—a sentiment to which Thomas à Kempis gave classic expression:

> Jesus has now many lovers of his heavenly kingdom, but few bearers of his cross. . . . He finds many companions of his table, but few of his abstinence. . . . All desire to rejoice with him, but few are willing to endure anything for his sake. Many follow Jesus to the breaking of bread, but few to the drinking of the chalice of his passion (Bk II, ch. 11).

Before leaving the topic of soteriological language, I believe it only right to mention a recent effort to rehabilitate the language of *satisfaction* which St. Anselm's *Cur Deus Homo* gave to Christian theology. Anselm (c. 1033-1109) was the first writer to devote a treatise explicitly to the atonement. His soteriology won wide endorsement from theologians in the Middle Ages, during the Reformation and later. Although few go as far as Adolf von Harnack ('no theory so bad had ever before his day been given out as ecclesiastical'), some twentieth-century scholars have dismissed talk of satisfaction as foreign to contemporary insights and treated Anselm himself as little more than an interesting survivor from a theological disaster area. It became customary to label his theory as Roman, legalistic and engrossed with the divine honour rather than the divine love.

However, John McIntyre, Gispert Greshake and now Walter Kasper have argued for the subtlety and splendour of Anselm's theology of satisfaction. This version of the atonement appreciates God's *fidelity* to creation and the moral order in a way that parallels St. Paul's sense of divine 'righteousness' (Rom 1, 17 etc.). Taken within the feudal context, the divine honour implies rather than excludes love. For Anselm 'honour' guarantees peace, order and justice. Lastly, his view of the atonement reflects the Germanic rather than the Roman culture and customs. Kasper has shown himself favourable to this fresh estimate of *Cur Deus Homo*.[46] But Küng, his colleague at the University of Tübingen, repeats the well-worn criticisms of Anselm's theology of satisfaction.[47]

Salvation from What?

Kasper and Küng also differ as regards the lostness from which Christ's saving work delivers men and women. Both take time out to ask in depth: What keeps the questions of salvation and redemption alive today? Both recognise evil as that present reality and profound mystery from which we yearn to be saved. Evil includes human sin but goes beyond it. (In parenthesis we can note how the pair from Tübingen prove here much superior to Pannenberg. He cannot really handle soteriology because he has not sufficiently faced the problem of evil. Pannenberg has frankly admitted this gap in his theology: 'The role played by sin, evil, suffering, destruction and brokenness in human history has not received very extensive treatment in my writings.'[48]) Where Kasper and Küng pull apart is over the setting in which they choose to talk about human liberation from evil.

Kasper quickly informs his readers that 'the crisis of meaning in modern society' is 'the place where Christology becomes relevant beyond the narrow context of theology'. The background to this crisis he traces through a list of German writers: Novalis, Fichte, Schelling, Hegel, Nietzsche and Heidegger. These and other authors indicate the way meaningless nihilism has come to threaten us.[49] Here Kasper takes a very European attitude towards the lostness from which Christ promises to rescue us. At least at this point he bypasses the demonic 'crises' produced by hunger, drugs, corrupt government, new forms of international exploitation, exploding cities, the systematic use of torture, massacres in Cambodia, civil war in Lebanon, and all the other horrors perpetrated by human fear and greed. To be sure, Kasper gives 'liberation' a key place in his soteriology and rightly remarks that any discussion of

Jesus Christ must try to relate 'a Christian understanding of redemption and a modern understanding
of emancipation'.[50] Nevertheless, he writes for North
Atlantic readers or—more accurately—for Europe-
ans who hunger for meaning but find a banal world
without and an emptiness within.[51] Kasper fails to
reflect on the questions of salvation, the crisis of
meaning and the sense of lostness which might be
alive today in Africa, India, Latin America, and the
New China of Mao Tse-tung. Or are we to suppose
that the 'crisis of meaning' in contemporary Europe
is paradigmatic for the rest of the world?

Küng does better. At the outset his eye runs
from Leningrad to Tashkent, to New Delhi and
Bangkok and then on to Tokyo and Melbourne.[52]
He then gives his interpretation of Christianity and
Christ a wide context which embraces Hinduism and
other major religions, various forms of Marxism and
that whole world which modern technology is fash-
ioning almost everywhere. At times Küng's comments may leave some readers outraged. Thus he
takes up Jesus' 'good news to the poor', observes
that 'everyman' meets 'the temptation to live by
bread alone', and insists that Jesus preached 'to the
damned of this world' that 'beyond the satisfying of
economic needs they are—in a much deeper sense—
poor, miserable, exploited and needy'.[53] If I am well-
fed, well-housed and well-clothed, should I tell my
starving brothers that Jesus warned us against the
temptation to live by bread alone? Nevertheless, one
can only applaud Küng's thoroughgoing attempt to
situate his Christology, soteriology and whole ac-

count of Christian life within a world context. *Christ sein* sees him truly moving beyond the narrow horizons of 'mere' Church reform to present Jesus' challenge to universal human aspirations.

Küng takes a broad scale and chooses world guidelines in pursuing his intention to 'activate the memory of Jesus as the one who is *ultimately normative*'.[54] He wants to show that his first-century life, death and resurrection possesses a unique and universal value for human salvation. All the same, one may wonder whether he actually succeeds in producing satisfactory grounds for making such an absolute claim for Jesus. Küng seems to rest much of his case on a repeated contrast between Jesus and the founders of other religious movements. Set alongside Buddha, Mohammed, Moses and Confucius (who is consistently and correctly called Kung-futse), Jesus looks quite different.

He was not educated at court, as Moses apparently was. He was no son of a king like Buddha. Also he was no scholar and politician like Kung-futse, nor was he a rich merchant like Mohammed. Precisely because his origin was so insignificant, his lasting importance is so astonishing.[55]

Whether we look at Jesus' background, career, message or influence, he evades any comparison.

None of the great founders of religions worked in so narrow a field. None lived such an outrageously short time. None died so young. And yet what an effect [he had]! Every fourth human being, about a thousand million persons are called Christian. Numerically Christianity comes by a wide margin at the head of all world religions.[56]

Küng marshals expertly the historical data which make Jesus' person and influence appear startlingly different. But does he manage to get beyond facts to the level of *principle*? Millions of people believe Jesus to be 'ultimately normative' for their lives. But what justifies their faith? Historical research gives Küng a stick with which to beat those who would glibly line Jesus up with a standard set of religious figures who have shaped world history. However, does Jesus differ from Buddha, Mohammed, Moses and the rest not merely *de facto*, but also *de iure*? Do we face simply a difference of degree but not one of kind?

I take it that these comparisons function *apologetically*. They prepare readers to move beyond the historical phenomena to accept in faith the *theological* basis for seeing Jesus as ultimately normative. That basis Küng locates, as Pannenberg and others do, in the events of Good Friday and Easter Sunday. The resurrection puts an absolute stamp of divine approval on the life of Jesus. Despite the shameful crucifixion, the cause of Jesus turns out to be truly the cause of God. Deciding for or against Jesus is nothing less than deciding for or against God. The crucified and risen Jesus personifies the final divine commitment to the world. He offers a definitive answer to the ultimate issues of life, including the questions of suffering and death.[57]

So far this article has been sampling contemporary reflections on the redemptive 'work' of Jesus Christ. For the most part it has been a matter of raising questions rather than presenting developed conclusions. One vast theme has been barely touched upon—the nature of salvation. Küng urges that 'being saved' is nothing other than being radically and genuinely human. In *Jesus* Schillebeeckx uses the traditional terminology of 'salvation', suggests that it amounts to what we mean by 'humanisation', and promises to write a soteriology for our times. This is clearly an urgent task. Those who seek to reunite Christology with soteriology will prove successful only if they confront the serious and decisive problems buried in the word 'salvation'. How does one explain today what Jesus Christ saves us for?

4
Commitment to Jesus

This book has tossed around the names of big-league exegetes and theologians: Brown, Kasper, Küng, Moltmann, Pannenberg, Schillebeeckx, Schoonenberg, Schürmann and Vawter. But the scholars cannot be allowed to have it all their own way when we examine the current thinking about Jesus.

A book written with the verve and vigour of Muggeridge's *Jesus* can tempt us to feel that technical theology and critical exegesis at times lets us down. This popular writer recaptures something scholars often prevent readers from seeing: that religious dimension of Jesus' story which demands our commitment.

Historical Scholarship

It takes, of course, no great effort to rustle up sweeping criticisms against the methods of a Muggeridge. He uses John's gospel as if it were a reliable historical source, indulges wild anachronisms, and largely ignores two centuries of biblical scholarship which have laid bare the processes behind the formation of the New Testament texts. Despite (or because of?) his being somewhat fundamentalist, however, Muggeridge discerns and describes a person fit to be the object of our faith. His Jesus is genuinely 'believable'.

But where do the so-called 'strictly historical' techniques take us? They may entail analysing texts, dismantling beliefs and carrying on minute debates in such a way that the Jesus of the gospels suffers the death of a thousand comments and details. It often seems futile looking for Jesus and his message in the official journals of New Testament studies. In the mid-1960s I trotted off one summer and attended an international scripture conference at an ancient university. The vice-chancellor, a lawyer by profession, had been asked to welcome the overseas visitors and open proceedings. A conscientious person, he prepared himself for the occasion by reading several commentaries on the gospels. He became baffled by the scholarly passion for dismembering the New Testament texts and preventing them from speaking for themselves. He mentioned this. Then slightly outraged and greatly puzzled he added: 'But these are good books! There's no need to treat them like that!' Muggeridge is not slow to hold up his hand in horror at 'the deserts and jungles of Biblical criticism'.[58] He derides the scholarship which has produced rows of new translations: 'Future historians . . . are likely to conclude that the more we knew about Jesus the less we knew him, and the more precisely his words were translated the less we understood or heeded them.'[59]

All of this borders dangerously on an irrational plea for the heart rather than the head, a preference for the 'simple' faith of the French peasant over the complexities of the German professor. Nevertheless, set Muggeridge's *Jesus* alongside Vawter's *This Man Jesus* and the contrast is startling. Vawter's book is technically correct and shows up the fundamentalist mistakes of the brilliant amateur, Muggeridge. The blurb on the cover claims that 'this book . . . offers all believers help in their desire to be in authentic contact with the living Christ and embrace his message in the light in which it was first proclaimed'. I wonder how many have accepted the offered help. Vawter's book has not proved nearly as successful as Muggeridge's in bringing believers—or for that matter non-believers—into authentic contact with the living Christ. Why is such New Testament scholarship failing? Or *pace* the blurb, does *This Man Jesus* properly remain at one remove from religious commitment and need to be 'applied' pastorally before it directly affects the life of faith?

Vawter himself remarks: 'The route of the historical method is admittedly not an easy one, and not everyone will always agree exactly where it leads.'[60] It is in fact high time to blow the whistle on the folly which can seem to turn this method into a latter-day idol. Some authors risk alleging that their use of historical techniques establishes contact with Jesus in a uniquely privileged way. Küng, for instance, contrasts 'the traditional' Jesus with 'the original' Jesus, compares the work of the critical scholar with that of an art expert, and concludes that the expert may uncover an original masterpiece which later hands have unwittingly painted over. Likewise 'it could come to light what the Church and theology have made out of Jesus and done with him—liturgically, dogmatically, politically, juridically and pedagogically'.[61]

Küng betrays here the enthusiasm for a brand of historical exegesis that so often mars as well as makes some recent Roman Catholic theology. To begin with, do we find Jesus by studying history rather than by participating in liturgy and persevering in scriptural meditation? Can exegesis assure us of some strikingly privileged contact with Jesus, denied to St. Francis of Assisi, St. Teresa of Avila and others unfortunate enough to live before the historical-critical method came along to uncover God's masterpiece? Secondly, Küng at this point lays claim to a fresh objectivity over against all that 'the Church and theology have made out of Jesus and done with him'. But what does the theologian Küng make out of Jesus and do with him? Should any theologian pretend to occupy a 'wiser-than-thou' position that puts him above and beyond the Church and other theologians?

Küng, however, goes on to allow that faith in Jesus does not depend upon the historical method.[62] At the end of the day he may in fact be highlighting only two functions of this method. First, it has the apologetic role of answering those who challenge the amount of public information available about Jesus. Second, it tracks down events which generated the New Testament texts. This grappling with the visible order of things can only serve to present the humanity of Jesus in a clearer light.

Elsewhere, Küng helpfully remarks that truth should not be reduced to historical truth:

> In given circumstances poetry can catch the secret of nature and of man better than some ever so exact description or photograph . . . . Truth is not identical with facticity, and in particular not identical with historical truth. . . . Poetry, parable and legend . . . can communicate more relevant truth than an historical report.[63]

He then introduces a remarkably useful comparison between (a) the gospels as dramatic representations of history and (b) historical plays of Shakespeare like *Henry V*.[64] This comparison deserves development.

Before going to Stratford-upon-Avon, we might wonder how freely Shakespeare has used his sources. We could decide to satisfy our historical demon by investigating the actual story of Henry V. We could settle for ourselves a hard core of facts. But then it would be absurd to sit through a performance, noting down carefully every point where the playwright has modified the record for his artistic purposes. Critical history can likewise assure us about the basic structure of Jesus' story. Brown, Kasper, Küng, Vawter and many others endorse a common consensus which takes Matthew, Mark and Luke to be substantially reliable in reporting what Jesus said and did. Having pacified our historical itch, we can then take up a gospel as a dramatic whole. It frames the story of Jesus and invites our involvement in a way in which, of course, *Henry V* does not. The gospel narratives will come alive for us, if we allow ourselves to come alive in the face of the texts. It may seem 'safer' to stick to a quest for historical details. But that way we will not truly find anything out—neither about Jesus nor about ourselves.

In brief, let the methods of critical history have their role, a subordinate rather than a dominant one. Sheer historical research can in fact turn out to be a way of avoiding the real drama and the essential issue raised by the gospels: Am I willing to put my whole life—with all its fears and hopes—into the crucified hands of Jesus? Any biblical research that finally prevents this challenge from being heard is both playing false to the nature of the gospels and substituting scholarly idols for the questions: 'What do you seek? Do you love me?' (Jn 1, 38; 21, 15).

Imagination and Commitment

Muggeridge's *Jesus* reminds us sharply that we are not saved by historical scholarship alone. A book that can be technically faulted by professional exegetes turns out to be religiously compelling. The reproductions of masterpieces which accompany the text suggest that sometimes we may approach Jesus more effectively through the imagination of artists rather than through the intellect of theologians. Muggeridge overstates his case to make this point: 'Only mystics, clowns and artists, in my experience, speak the truth, which, as Blake was always insisting, is perceptible to the imagination rather than the mind.'[65] Our knowledge of Jesus Christ is far too serious a business to be left to theologians and exegetes alone. From the Middle Ages these professionals have monotonously neglected art and the imagination as guides to religious truth. I find myself in complete agreement with those who wish to reinstate the 'mystics, clowns and artists' alongside the scholars. The imaginable is the believable. To modify Wittgenstein: What we cannot imagine, we must confine to silence and non-belief.

Finally, Muggeridge rests his case on the mutual dependence of commitment and knowledge. St. Augustine's 'Give me a lover and he will understand' applies here. A genuine moral sensibility and a true religious concern make it possible to know and understand Jesus. After all the criticisms are in, only the mean-minded can overlook the deep attachment to Jesus which lights up page after page of *Christ sein*. The enormous success of Küng's book derives at least partly from this affectionate commitment to Jesus and his cause. The Swiss theologian published *Christ sein* on the twentieth anniversary of his priestly ordination. 'This book', he insisted at the press conference, 'was not written because the author considers himself a good Christian, but because he thinks that being a Christian is a particularly good thing.' Muggeridge goes further than Küng in admitting his personal sinfulness. It makes him unworthy of the Lord. Yet this gives him an ultimate claim on the one who 'came not to call the righteous, but sinners' (Mk 2, 17). Does Muggeridge's *Jesus* verify at the level of popular writing the need for that multi-layered conversion which Bernard Lonergan has championed? Should we adapt Augustine and exclaim, 'Give me a repentant and prayerful theologian and he or she will understand Jesus'?

At the end of the day, it may be nothing less than the praise of forgiven sinners which will find the right language to use of Jesus Christ, the one who died that we might live.

Appendix:
The Imagination of Jesus

For some people Christmas can act as an irritating reminder that we know so little about the life of Jesus—except for some crowded months at the end. Once his ministry begins, we see him delivering his unique message, healing the sick, pardoning sinners and—as the opposition gathers with stunning speed—quickly becoming a man on the run. Action fills that last year or two. But before then Jesus lives through three decades about which we know next to nothing. We can be haunted by our incredibly slight information about his birth, childhood, youth and early manhood.

Some Christians coped with their bewilderment by giving their fantasies free rein and inventing answers to all the questions we or others might care to ask. The so-called apocryphal gospels did their best to fill in the details about all those blanks in Jesus' life.

When the Holy Family arrived in Egypt, one account informs us that the temple idols crashed in pieces before the baby Jesus and that Pharaoh himself recognised him as truly God. The apocryphal gospels chatter on also about the silent years in Nazareth. Some of these stories may seem mere pious imaginings, but others can be downright nasty. One story portrays Jesus walking through a village when a child runs into him. Jesus curses him and the child dies on the spot. The people of the village complain to Joseph, telling him to leave at once as their children are in danger. When Joseph passes on the complaint to Jesus, the villagers who complained are struck blind. Joseph sees what has happened, seizes Jesus' ear and gives it a good tug. The last point in the story can seem amusing. But the whole narrative exudes a taste for spiteful and murderous magic. Here, as elsewhere, we can appreciate that the Christian Church did well to refuse to accept such apocryphal gospels into the canon of the New Testament.

But are we simply left then to put up with our very limited knowledge about so much of Jesus' life? Not altogether. Some conclusions can be legitimately drawn from the first three gospels. There his preaching offers some clues as to *the way in which his imagination formed during the years in Nazareth*. The language and imagery used by Jesus hints at the way he perceived the world.

Four Presuppositions

Before developing this argument and exploring the imagery of Jesus, I should clarify some presuppositions.

(1) I am not holding that *all* the language which Matthew, Mark and Luke attribute to Jesus neces-

sarily goes back to the actual ministry. Some of that
language derives from the gospel writers themselves,
from the early Church traditions or from the risen
Christ himself.

(2) I am not claiming that the gospel writers
ever give us an exact transcript of the words Jesus
used. But I agree with many scholars that Matthew,
Mark and Luke present *a substantially accurate version* of what Jesus said. In what follows I wish to
refer only to those passages which seem to come
from his preaching—in their general drift, if not necessarily in their precise wording. That degree of
reliability suffices for our purposes. A pattern of
images can come through, even where verbal expres-
sions may fluctuate and change somewhat.

(3) Beyond question, Jesus used some expressive language which others had provided. He inherit-
ed a rich and diverse storehouse of imagery which he
could adopt and creatively employ. The imagery
drawn from the past appeared both to liberate—not
block—his originality and to serve his strongly individual style of preaching. Nevertheless, I am not trying here to assess his degree of originality. The question is *not*: How uniquely inventive did Jesus show
himself in his language? Rather my question is:
What does the imagery used by Jesus suggest about
the way his sensibility functioned?

(4) Let me add a final remark for readers nervous about orthodoxy. I am not discussing, let alone
calling into question, Jesus' divine identity. All the
same, no appeal to his status as the Word of God
become flesh will tell us anything significant about

the actual ways in which his human imagination operated. We may get some clues about that from the material in the gospels.

Features of Jesus' Imagination

After noting these major presuppositions, let us come back to the case being argued. The preaching of Jesus lets us glimpse the flow and flavour of the imagination which took shape during the hidden life at Nazareth. We can pick out four features of his imagery.

(1) First, Jesus shows himself aware of and responsive to *a broad range of human activity, suffering and happiness.* He notes how farmers fatten calves for a feast, and knows that bumper harvests may call for extra barns. If he offers no suggestions about thistle control and the removal of rocks, he realizes that poor terrain can reduce the results of seeding. He recalls how people arrange parties, organise ceremonies and behave at feasts. He has watched people putting patches on torn cloaks and using fresh wineskins for new wine. Jesus knows, too, popular ways for forecasting the weather: 'When you see a cloud rising in the west, you say at once, "A shower is coming"; and so it happens. And when you see the south wind blowing, you say, "There will be scorching heat"; and so it happens' (Lk 12, 5ff).

Jesus does not flinch from facing human suffering. One of his most memorable stories features a traveler who is robbed, beaten up and left half-dead on a country roadside. He points to the greed of rich men which allows them to over-indulge, although sick beggars may lie starving in the streets outside. Human happiness does not pass Jesus by: the joy of a father whose renegade son returns, the celebrations at weddings, a housewife delighted to have recovered some missing money.

All in all, Jesus speaks of a wide range of human activity: the role of stewards in large households, the administration of the law, the price of sparrows in the market, the right recipe for mixing yeast with flour, poor building practices, financial investments, and much else besides. *The language of Jesus suggests an imagination that has scanned a great deal of normal human living.* If we gathered together all his images, we would have a reasonably detailed sketch of daily life in ancient Galilee.

(2) The preaching of Jesus tells the story of his imagination in a second way. His sensibility seems to have its *preferences.* He uses, for instance, a large number of farming images, which may seem surprising. He draws many illustrations, not from carpentry, but from agriculture and the care of cattle. He knows that donkeys and oxen need to be taken every day to water. These animals at times fall down wells and must be rescued even on the sabbath. Jesus notes that cultivating the soil and adding fertiliser might revitalise a barren fig tree. Farmers may buy up to five yoke of oxen. Gentile farmers keep pigs and feed them on pods. Piling up manure heaps, growing mulberry trees, gathering crops from the

fields, separating wheat from darnel, minding sheep, ploughing the land—references to these and other farming activities dot the preaching of Jesus.

(3) For the most part, Jesus reveals an imagination that has grown to be sensitively aware of what is going on in his world. Nevertheless, there are *some gaps in the picture*. And this is my third point about his imagery. He delights in children, but he has next to nothing to say about the mother-child relationship. Occasionally he glances at the father-child relationship: 'What father among you, if his son asks him for a fish, will instead of a fish give him a serpent; or if he asks for an egg will give him a scorpion?' (Lk 11, 11f). But Jesus somehow finds his way round the mother-child relationship almost without pausing to notice it. When his eye runs forward to the troubles to come, he sympathises over the sufferings that will afflict pregnant women and nursing mothers: 'Alas for women with child in those days, and for those who have children at the breast' (Mk 13, 17). Except for one or two such tangential remarks, Jesus bypasses the mother-child relationship. Did he have such an utterly untroubled relationship to his own mother that this intimate area of life produced nothing for his language? Does it take the 'grit' of some tension in such areas to produce imaginative pearls? Whatever the reason, his preaching does not derive imagery from the mother-child relationship.

Almost as remarkable is his silence about the husband-wife relationship. He defends married life by rejecting divorce, and insisting that even in their minds men should not go lusting after other men's wives. He speaks of marriage feasts, wedding guests and the maidens who waited for the bridegroom to fetch his bride from her parents' home to his own. But there the imagery stops. Nothing survives from the preaching of Jesus about the loving and caring life together of married people. To illustrate the nature of prayer Jesus tells a story about troubling one's neighbour at midnight to borrow some food:

> Which of you who has a friend will go to him at midnight and say to him: 'Friend, lend me three loaves; for a friend of mine has arrived on a journey, and I have nothing to set before him'; and he will answer from within: 'Do not bother me; the door is now shut, and my children are with me in bed; I cannot get up and give you anything'? I tell you, though he will not get up and give him anything because he is his friend, yet because of his importunity he will rise and give him whatever he needs (Lk 11, 5-8).

We might have expected the story to run: 'Do not bother me. The door is now shut, and my wife is with me in bed.' But Jesus has the man say: 'My children are with me in bed.'

Jesus differs from the scriptures he knows by not drawing images from the mother-child and husband-wife relationships. Isaiah, the psalms and other Old Testament books made childbirth a common

simile: 'Like a woman with child, who writhes and
cries out in her pangs, when she is near her time, so
were we because of thee, O Lord' (Is 26, 17). Such
imagery moves with natural ease to depict nursing
mothers and growing babies:

> Rejoice with Jerusalem, and be glad for her,
> all you who love her. . . .
> You shall suck, you shall be carried upon her
>   hip,
> and dandled upon her knees.
> As one whom his mother comforts,
> so I will comfort you (Is 66, 10-12).

The husband-wife relationship likewise turns up
frequently among Old Testament images—particularly to focus the disobedience of God's people.
Their idolatry and other sins grieved Yahweh as a
wife's infidelities grieve her husband. The sacred
writers also saw the positive possibilities in this comparison. Hosea celebrates God as the tender lover
who longs to woo his people. But none of this appears in the gospel record.

Besides the mother-child and husband-wife relationship, there are other facets of human life that fail
to get reflected in the language and imagery of Jesus.
He refers to the ravens and the lilies, goes to the wil-
derness to pray and climbs mountains with his disciples. Nevertheless, his preaching reveals no delight in
nature and natural beauty. Nor does he indulge any

pathos at the transience of things. He is so busy urging his audience to live like genuine children of God that he has no time to indulge wistful sadness at the world—still less disillusionment with it. He could never make Vergil's sentiment his own: 'There are tears for human affairs and mortal things touch the mind *(sunt lacrimae rerum et mentem mortalia tangunt)*.' Admittedly Jesus weeps over Jerusalem and shakes his head sadly: 'O Jerusalem, Jerusalem, killing the prophets and stoning those who are sent to you! How often would I have gathered your children together as a hen gathers her brood under her wings, and you would not' (Lk 13, 34). But, by and large, Jesus says little about his own failures and perplexities.

Finally, images drawn from history, current world affairs and geography hardly surface in the preaching of Jesus. There is a hereness and nowness about his language, a preoccupation with the scene right in front of him. He recalls, of course, a few episodes from biblical history or myth like the story of the flood and the destruction of Sodom. But Jesus betrays little interest in the past. He never mentions that founding event of Jewish history, the exodus from Egypt. The Maccabean revolt, the Hasmonean period, the capture of Jerusalem by Pompey, the switch of Jewish allegiance to Julius Caesar, the reign of Herod the Great (37-4 B.C.) and all the other crowded events of recent history never even got a passing nod in Jesus' preaching. That larger world of politics fails to come in sight. Apart from a brief remark about paying taxes to Caesar and a comment on some victims of Pilate's brutality, Jesus hardly even suggests that he is living under Roman rule. Once he draws a lesson from a military build-up—the king with ten thousand troops deciding not to risk war against a king with twenty thousand troops. But Jesus names no specific king nor any particular cold-war situation in the Mediterranean world of the first century. Another time he speaks vaguely of 'a nobleman' who 'went into a far country to receive kingly power and then return' (Lk 19, 12). But he mentions no historical figure as the peg onto which he hangs the parable of the pounds that follows. Jesus' mind reaches out to the immediate situation here and now. He neither scans history, not even the most recent history, nor lets his eye run around the Roman Empire for images and examples that he could press into service.

At times the message of Ezekiel and other classic prophets takes us around the world of their day: Persia, Egypt, Cyprus, Tarshish, Greece, southern Russia and a range of other places. But the known geography of his day provides little or no imagery for Jesus. His preaching does not even suggest that he lived near the Mediterranean.

To sum up: There is a hereness and a nowness about the language of Jesus, a preoccupation with the scene right in front of him. He does not share in that romantic imagination which revels in ancient times and far-away places.

So much for my third observation that the language of Jesus did not represent the whole of the world in which he lived. One could, of course, argue that his preaching did actually introduce historical references, included imagery drawn from the mother-child relationship and so forth. But the early Church and/or the evangelists censored out nearly all this language. One can only respond, however, that there are no plausible reasons for believing that such censorship took place. In general, we do best to work with what we have rather than speculate about missing material.

(4) Fourth, we throw away any right to comment on the way Jesus perceives reality, if we ignore *the earthy particularity* of his language. Characteristically, he answers general questions like 'Who is my neighbour?' by telling a story (Lk 10, 29-37). Of course, other rabbis have done that—both before and after Jesus. But the fact that they can also display this habit does not make it any less his own. He thinks from below, not by way of deduction from above. He offers cases from which his audience can draw general principles if they want to. Even his generalising remarks stay close to earth: 'No one after drinking old wine desires new' (Lk 5, 39). There is a common touch in the proverbial sayings he cites: 'Doubtless you will quote to me this proverb: "Physician, heal yourself"' (Lk 4, 23). He invites his hearers to perceive the particular things around them. His imagery is attuned to the earthy wisdom of ordinary people. All of this makes him the supreme preacher with the common touch. He speaks with us and to us, not merely at us.

To conclude: The imagery and language that Jesus uses suggests at least four conclusions about his sensibility. (1) A very wide range of things in his immediate environment catch his eye. If he is intensely aware of God, he also seems intensely aware of what he experiences on the human scene. (2) He has his preferences among the things he observes. (3) There are some surprising gaps in what he appears to notice. (4) His mind works from below—from the concrete case. In his own unique way he betrays the earthy wisdom of ordinary people.

The apocryphal gospels of early Christianity reflected popular curiosity about the hidden years of Jesus' life and indulged the imagination of their readers. It is more to the point, however, to reflect on Jesus' own imagination. The imagery that he employed gives a clue to the way his perception of the world worked. To move through his language to some insights into his sensibility can only be a real gain.

Notes

1. W. Kasper, *Jesus der Christus* (Mainz, 1974), p. 26 (=*Jesus the Christ* [New York, 1976] p. 24; hereafter ET).

2. *Ibid.*, p. 44 (= ET, p. 37).

3. *The Man for Others* (London, 1964), p. ix.

4. In *The Christ* (London, 1972) Schoonenberg develops at length the difficulties that he (and others) find in the Chalcedonian pattern—at least as classical theology has understood it. See also 'Is Jesus "man plus God"?' *Theology Digest* 23 (1975), pp. 59-70.

5. *Christ sein*, p. 336 (=*On Being a Christian* [New York, 1976], p. 347; hereafter ET).

6. *Philosophical Fragments* (Princeton, 1962), p. 130.

7. *The Christ*, p. 63.

8. *Christ sein*, pp. 15ff. and 109ff. (= ET, pp. 25ff., 119ff.). See K. Rahner and W. Thüsing, *Christologie—systematisch und exegetisch* (Freiburg, 1972).

9. Paris, 1968 & 1972.

10. K. Rahner, 'On the Theology of the Incarnation', *Theological Investigations* 4 (London, 1974), p. 110.

11. *Christ sein*, p. 437 (= ET, p. 447).

12. *Jezus* (Bloemendaal, 1974), p. 545.

13. *Theological Investigations* 4, pp. 130, 185; *Theological Dictionary* (New York, 1965), p. 402.

14. *The Human Face of God* (London, 1973), p. 148.

15. *Christ sein*, pp. 120-22; cf. p. 136 (= ET, pp. 128-30; cf. p. 144).

16. *Ibid.*, pp. 137-66 (= ET, pp. 145-74).

17. *Ibid.*, p. 152 (= ET, p. 160).

18. Luke describes Paul's encounter with the risen

Lord on the Damascus road in 'heavenly', glorious terms. That meeting is quite unlike the meeting with the two disciples on the Emmaus road (Lk 24, 13-35).

19. *Christ sein*, pp. 342f. (= ET, p. 353f.).

20. *Ibid.*, pp. 446f. (= ET, p. 456f.).

21. 'The Problem of the Virginal Conception of Jesus', *The Virginal Conception and Bodily Resurrection of Jesus* (New York, 1973), pp. 21-68.

22. *Ibid.*, pp. 66f.

23. In *The Easter Jesus* (London, 1973) I argue that 'with respect to resurrection faith, sheer reason and good sense alone fail to prove decisive' (p. 137; cf. pp. 63-74).

24. *This Man Jesus* (New York, 1973), p. 134; italics mine.

25. *Christ sein*, pp. 150f. (= ET, pp. 158-60).

26. *This Man Jesus*, pp. 13ff.

27. *Christ sein*, pp. 325ff. (= ET, pp. 335ff.).

28. See further the Appendix, 'The Imagination of Jesus'.

29. *Jesus der Christus*, p. 25 (=ET, p. 24).

30. *Christ sein*, p. 438 (= ET, p. 448).

31. *Jesus—God and Man* (London, 1968), p. 350.

32. *Jesus* (London, 1975), p. 135; italics mine.

33. *Jesu ureigener Tod* (Freiburg, 1975), pp. 16-65. The author documents abundantly the recent German literature on the theme.

34. *This Man Jesus*, p. 80; italics mine.

35. This terminology comes from Kasper, *Jesus der Christus*, p. 141 (=ET, p. 120). It is also used by Schürmann and others.

36. *Jesus the Jew* (London, 1973), p. 224.

37. *Jezus* (Bloemendaal, 1974), p. 256.

38. Raymond E. Brown, *Crises Facing the Church* (London, 1975), pp. 34-36.

39. *Jesus der Christus*, p. 141 (=ET, p. 120).

40. *Christ sein*, pp. 175-83 (= ET, pp. 183-91).

41. *Jesus der Christus*, pp. 47f. (=ET, pp. 42f.).

42. *Ibid.*, p. 242 (=ET, pp. 205f.).

43. *Christ sein*, p. 381 (= ET, p. 391).

44. *Jesus der Christus*, pp. 256f. (=ET, pp. 216f.).

45. *Ibid.*, p. 256 (=ET, p. 216).

46. *Ibid.*, pp. 260ff. (= ET, pp. 219ff.).

47. *Christ sein,* pp. 411f. and 653 (= ET, pp. 421ff. and 666).

48. Postscript to E. Frank Tupper, *The Theology of Wolfhart Pannenberg* (London, 1974), p. 303.

49. *Jesus der Christus*, p. 15 (=ET, p. 16).

50. *Ibid.*, p. 48 (=ET, p. 43).

51. *Ibid.*, pp. 14f. (=ET, pp. 16f.).

52. *Christ sein,* p. 31 (= ET, p. 40).

53. *Ibid.*, p. 260 (= ET, p. 270f.).

54. *Ibid.*, p. 116 (= ET, p. 124).

55. *Ibid.*, p. 203 (= ET, p. 212).

56. *Ibid.*, p. 142; see pp. 269, 273, 324, 334, 427, etc. (= ET, p. 150; see pp. 278, 283, 334, 345, 436f.).

57. *Ibid.*, pp. 371-400, 418-26 (= ET, pp. 381-410, 428-36).

58. *Jesus,* p. 74.

59. *Ibid.*, p. 8.

60. *This Man Jesus*, p. 28.

61. *Christ sein,* p. 152 (= ET, p. 166).

62. *Ibid.*, p. 153 (= ET, p. 161).

63. *Ibid.*, pp. 405f. (= ET, p. 415f.).

64. *Ibid.*, p. 407 (= ET, p. 416f.).

65. *Jesus,* p. 37.